How to Become a Stock-Picking Pro

Learn Stock Picking Strategies That the Masters Use

Jason Mitchell

Jason Mitchell Publishing
1501 Balsam Drive
New Windsor, NY 12553

Ordering Information:
Quantity sales. Special discounts are available on quantity purchases by corporations, associations, and others. For details, contact the publisher at the address above.
Orders by U.S. trade bookstores and wholesalers. Please contact Big Distribution: jakm86@gmail.com

Printed in the United States of America

First Edition

14 13 12 11 10 / 10 9 8 7 6 5 4 3 2 1

Table of Contents

Introduction

What comes to mind when you think about getting rich and building wealth?

What do you think when I ask you how the top 1% make and keep their money?

The chances that you said stocks are very high, and there is a reason for that. Outside or Real Estate and Business, the stock market is the biggest wealth creator in the world today.

It is easy to see why stocks are seen as the great moneymaker. It is so liquid you can get money in and out at less time than dinner takes to make. Of course, if you are not careful in that same time you can lose your shirt.

In this book, I want to share with you some of the most popular ways of finding great stocks…and some great ways to avoid the bad ones.

So we will look at certain disciplines of stock picking by each given area of expertise. Each discipline is used by certain investors to attain the great pleasure of not only outpacing inflation and make more money than they lose, but to also beat the S&P 500 benchmark that all professionals and even non-professionals strive to do.

Now before we dig into these great stock-picking guidelines I need to make sure you understand something…

There is no way to not lose money…besides maybe doing nothing at all. But that means you still lose, money cause banks never pay enough interest to outpace inflation consistently.

So get proactive and do something, or DIE!

Back to my point…

If you bought this book in hopes that you were going to find some magic pill to picking the right stocks all of the time, and make money all of the time I am sorry if one exist I haven't found it. And I talk to professional investors, entrepreneurs, business owners, and other people with money all the time.

Even the greatest investors and entrepreneurs lose money…some more than you would think.

The key is to cut your losers fast, let your winners run, and know the difference.

You will lose money, but you must win more than you lose and that means have discipline and patience to make this work.

I hate when I lose money to, but it happens. Especially when investing for my clients, but that is the game we play. My goal is to make more than I lose…PERIOD!

That is the best that anyone can expect of you.

There are some reasons as to why no stock picking strategy will win 100% of the time. It is the reason why I run a flexible fund or better known as a multi-strategy firm…it's to take advantage of the changing times we are in, and never be without a way to make money.

This works for me seeing how I am paid mostly on results. When you have to kill to eat you, get over yourself real fast, and do what works.

Some of the reasons no stock picking strategy works is:

1. There are factors affecting a company that no one can count on. All you can do is collect the data and do your very best.

2. When dealing with people you can expect things to be irrational. Now take myself for instance...I try to be rational and I do a good job, but it isn't easy when you have real money on the line. Even I have to remind myself to be strong and not get emotionally involved.
3. A lot of information is not measurable and is intangible. Profits are easy to measure, but measuring the effectiveness of staff and reputation and goodwill are very hard.

What you will also find is that two drastically different stock picking strategies will work at the same time. You should also look at personal goals, risk tolerance, time frame, and how much time you have to invest.

If you can get good at this you can easily multiply your paycheck and get to a place where you can be very well off, to rich, to very rich, to wealthy. The ball is in your court. You get to decide.

Now most of these disciplines are under the umbrella of fundamental analysis. The last one is about technical analysis. If you don't know what that means don't worry...you will find out soon.

But know that all it really is, is finding a company that you can invest in and determining the worth of said company.

Fundamental Analysis

What does it mean when you hear someone say the company has "strong/weak fundamentals"? It has become a bit of a word we throw around, and it loses meaning.

I hear professional money managers, brokers, and analyst refer to a company's fundamentals and say nothing at all.

I want to talk about why starting at fundamental analysis is a great way to find companies; what fundamentals actually are comprised of, and why and how they are analyzed.

Concepts

Fundamental analysis is easier and more straightforward than you might think. All it takes is a little time to do the work.

When doing fundamental analysis the key is to find the intrinsic value (just a fancy word for net worth) of the company. Your job is to find out what the company is really worth as opposed to what it is trading for on the stock market.

So if the intrinsic value is more than the current share price that could be a perfect sign that this is a company worth buying.

There are many ways to try to find out a company's intrinsic value…the fact is that they are all ways to do one thing: find the company's discounted cash flow, because the sum of a company is it's discounted cash flow.

Discounted Cash Flow?

A valuation method used to estimate the attractiveness of an investment opportunity.

Discounted cash flow (DCF) analysis uses future free cash flow projections and then discounts them (most often using the weighted average cost of capital) to arrive at a present value, which is used to evaluate the potential for investment.

If the value arrived at through DCF analysis is higher than the current cost of the investment, the opportunity may be a good one.

Calculated as:

$$DCF = \frac{CF_1}{(1+r)^1} + \frac{CF_2}{(1+r)^2} + \ldots + \frac{CF_n}{(1+r)^n}$$

CF = Cash Flow

r = discount rate (WACC)

Also known as the Discounted Cash Flows Model.

What this means very plainly is that a company is worth all of it's future profits. These future profits must be discounted to take into account the time value of money (another big fancy term that we will get to later).

An easy way to thinking about it is that $1 given to you a year from now, is worth a lot less than $1 given to you today.

Intrinsic value being equal to future profits makes perfect sense when you think about what a business gives its shareholders.

If you have a private company, you can get the money from the company year after year since there is no growth in stock price. The only way you can take out of a company is if it has money left over after paying salaries, cost of goods sold, inventory, equipment, etc.

There's a Sucka Born Every Minute

The problem with using the DCF model is that you must assume that people are rational and coherent. That nobody would every buy a business that is more than it's discounted cash flow.

WRONG!!!

Let's look at the stock market since most of you aren't in the position to buy a private business, either a percentage or wholly.

When you think about the stock market you have to realize that the prices can be volatile and differ greatly from what the underlying company is worth. Why is it like that? We know that the intrinsic value of the underlying company doesn't differ greatly from day to day, so why does the stock price?

The truth is that for many people stocks are just pieces of paper that you can buy at one price and sell to another buyer at hopefully a higher price. With this mindset no one cares about the cash flows, debt, or much of anything else.

This is called the greater fool theory.

It's called the greater fool theory because the profit is made when you buy a stock and sell it to another investor/trader for higher than you bought it. It doesn't take into account the company's value.

A trader would call the buyer a fool who just bases her decisions on fundamental analysis, because it doesn't take into account trends and current economic conditions. The investor would call the trader a fool cause in the long run a stock will reflect what a company is actually worth intrinsically.

A classic debate between someone who practices fundamental analysis and one who follows technical analysis.

Someone who is a technician (term used for a trader or someone who uses technical analysis as their primary stock picking strategy) does not care about value, worth, profits, or anything even about the business. They care about trends and making decisions based off of stock charts.

There is no way to say that fundamental or technical analysis is better than the other one. Each has its strengths and weaknesses. Technical analysis is seen as a short-term strategy, and fundamental analysis is seen as more of a long-term one.

Walk the Walk, & Talk the Talk

If anyone tells you that using DCF valuations is easy, please turn away from them and walk away. Walk away very fast.

That being said it isn't impossible to do…just not easy.

One problem of DCF is how far into the future can you project future cash flow. It is enough to decide how you are going to do next year, but to try to forecast 10 years into the future.

Any number of things can affect your projections. There could be a recession. The business could go out of business. Anything can happen that can and will affect the cash flow of a business from the next year going into the future ten.

All of the uncertainty and possible outcomes is exactly why there are so many different ways to get the job done. But none of it takes into consideration the complications posed by not knowing what will happen in the future.

Options

There are other methods of valuation.

You could analyze the net income, EBITDA, free cash flow, and other financial models.

There are pros and cons to each of these metrics to find out what the intrinsic value of a company would be.

Just know fundamental analysis is all about finding out what a company is actually worth vs. what the market is offering the company/shares for. It is all about the earnings (another term for cash flow).

When doing your fundamental analysis you need to get your tools so you can start doing the work. You need three documents to run the math and start checking to see if the company's intrinsic value is in line with what the stock market is offering it at, or even if the price it is being offered at privately.

You need the income statement, balance sheet, and cash flow statements. I like to work from 10 years from that year…5 for private businesses (they rarely have 10 years worth of numbers…hell they rarely have 5).

You can get those documents on finance.yahoo.com, thestreet.com, money.msn.com, or any other financial stock site.

Qualitative Analysis

When you are analyzing a company you are being "foolish" (see how I chose a nice way of saying it) if all you do is crunch the numbers. We also have to look at the more subjective elements of analyzing a company.

This is why this section is on qualitative analysis…it's because it relies on your intuition and you deciding what facts are important to you as an investor.

When it comes these metrics and factors it is all about your personal preference and tolerance level. Math is math and the numbers don't lie, but what do you do when you have to look at a company that you need to look at more than just the facts.

The C-Suite

When analyzing a company it is important to know who is making the decisions at the top. Who is making the day-to-day decisions that are dictating the decisions of the company.

When analyzing the management it is smart to start with WWWWW (who, what, where, when, and why). This way when you knock out all of the W's and you feel more confident in your assessment of the top.

Who

This is where you dig into who are the C-Suite team. By c-suite I mean CEO, CMO, CFO, CIO, and COO. Who are they?

You could go deeper into looking into who is in the Board of Directors also…at this point the more foundational work you do the better it all is to make your decisions in the future.

What

What is the strategic goals of the management company? What is the management philosophy? Are they mostly cut cost at any means necessary? Are they about giving their shareholders more value and increasing the value of the business for them?

You have to know how they manage the company. Some are very secretive and others very open. Do you have a Richard Branson or a Jack Welch? A Warren Buffet or a Steve Jobs?

Is the management style flexible and fluid…so they are better at adapting to the changes in the environment? Or, are they rigid and all emphasis is based on logic?

You can get a good sense of the management style by reading the annual report's management, discussion, and analysis section (MD&A). From there you can see if it fits the company.

Where

It is normally good to know where people come from.

What is their background? How did they get into the position they are in now?

You have to see if where they are from, makes you feel comfortable about where they are in the company's organizational structure.

Some only want managers that have experience in one given industry to be running that company. They feel weary about a tech CEO all of the sudden running an investment bank.

In most cases that should raise some alarms, but in others maybe not.

It goes back to the who question.

For some it would be dangerous cause they cannot adapt to the new position. But for someone like me who has worked with clients in over 400 industries and is always looking for what connects industries it wouldn't be too hard.

I've been and know of other entrepreneurs and investors who are in many industries over their career and even at the same time.

This is why the Who was first.

For example, Richard Branson is in many different industries under the Virgin Group, and we accept that from him…yet for some reason we wouldn't accept the same thing from someone like Lee Iacocca is someone we only see in the Auto Industry.

I like to also bring up musicians…no other group has shown a knack for diversifying their business and skill acumen from music to other industries than musicians.

But that being said why stress yourself hoping that they can deliver? If someone used to run a huge company, but is now running a start up in that industry it seems plausible they could handle the job.

On the other hand what about a CEO from the company that provides the seats for airplanes all of the sudden becoming the CEO of the airplane company? Is that too far a stretch?

It is all subjective.

When

So after you finish with Who, What, and When we can get to the When of it all.

When did this current C-Suite take over? In that when you should also find out how long they've been in the driver's seat and how the company stock and performance has been during that time period.

Sometimes a new CEO comes in at a bad time and performance goes down before they are able to get it back again.

We call these Macro Economic concerns.

So if the current management has been there for awhile that could be a good sign. When a company is doing poorly one of the first things shareholders and board of directors do is to oust the current management and get some new blood in the seat to try and do something different.

So a company that is always changing who sits in the big chair to me is a red flag. Why are they always changing the Suite? Are they giving management enough time? What are the conditions or problems the company is facing? How long can it last?

These are some of the questions you should ask yourself repeatedly until you can come up with some answers.

Management restructuring isn't always a bad thing. When Lee Iacocca took over Chrysler he changed up the management and it brought the bankrupt company to new heights and to the top of the pack.

So nothing is black and white. You have to take in all the information and be willing to change your mind when the facts change, or new ones are introduced. It's the only way to stay alive.

Why

Why have these people (or person if only one person has changed position…the most important normally is the CEO) been put in their current position?

Why them and not someone else?

Why are they right for the job? Why not them?

Sector, Industry, & Competition

Before we begin I want to say that what I mean by sector is the big picture or 50,000 view of the slice of economy the business is in.

For example are you in the financial sector, technology sector, utilities sector, etc.

Now Industry dig down and gets you a little more personal, so in the financial sector here are some industries:

- REITs
- Investment Companies/Asset Management
- Savings and Loans Banks
  - Regional
  - National
  - Local
- Investment Banks
  - Local
  - Regional
  - National
- Mutual Funds

I could do the same for the other sectors, but you get the point.

So when doing your research you should be able to answer if the company is in a growth industry, what effects the company's ability to make money is not always what affects the companies sector...not always.

(This is getting into secular growth stocks, cyclicals, and more classifications that we will tackle at another day and time.)

Where are we in the economy is also a consideration here. If the sector is in an upswing than even a mediocre company can do pretty good...though it is best to stick with the Best of Breed.

In this section we also have other things to consider. Some of them are (1) market share (meaning how much of a given market buys from you vs. your competitors…think Apple or Microsoft), and (2) barriers of entry, such as high start up cost.

What Did You Say You Do Again?

You'd be surprised how many people invest in a company and don't know what the hell it does or how it makes its money.

I'm always shocked by that…

Yes you can assume that a bank makes money from paying interest on money at one rate and lending it out at another and keeping the difference.

You can assume retailers sell products and make money from the difference of what they paid for it versus what they charge us.

But you can never be sure. This is why looking at the quarterly reports and even the annual reports is so important. Make sure that how the company makes money is how it makes money.

This is so easy it shouldn't need the time and energy to write it, but my experience has taught me that it needs bearing…and it needs it now.

You can always get people when you ask them how a company of the stock they bought makes money. They throw out all these fancy terms that sometimes you think they know what they are talking about.

I always say if a person who doesn't know or understand business cannot understand you, than you don't really know what you are saying. But if they can, especially if you can explain it to a 5 year old than you know what the company does and how it makes it money.

CONGRATS!!! ☺

It's All About The Brand

For some people the power of a brand is very important.

Think of such well-known brands such as: Coca-Cola, Pepsi, Boeing, and McDonalds.

These are all brands that to some are worth billions of dollars.

Thinking about a conglomerate of brands I think of Procter & Gamble and General Electric…also my mentor Warren Buffet's Berkshire Hathaway is essentially a collection of brands of different industries.

So Brand Equity is something that you as an investor will want to take into consideration when buying into a company.

Complicate Much

The worse thing to do is to turn this business into more work than it really is.

I get great investment ideas from my brothers or nieces and nephew who are tied into things more than I am. For example some of my plays with GameStop, and other retailers is solely from hearing them talk about their regular lives.

You have the same opportunity.

You'd be surprised what you can find out by talking to people and just keeping an open mind and keeping your options open.

The point is that Wall Street analyst aren't the only ones that can get access to information on a company. Sometimes people just going about their days can give you great insight.

I made a good profit on Nike when I overheard people telling me they couldn't even get into the stores to buy the sneakers they wanted…they had to be on some waiting list. I immediately did some digging and got to work.

In Conclusion

Looking at a company from a sales and earnings standpoint isn't enough. I love ratios as much as the next guy, but you need to do more.

Looking at the qualitative elements of a business is by far one of the easiest ways to evaluate a company, but don't take it for granted. It can also be one of the most effective.

Value Investing

Value investing is perhaps one of the best-known investing strategies in the world. Good reason for it too.

Its biggest rock star is Warren Buffet, and we know him to be the world's richest investor.

Let's take a minute to find out what this means…

It means he is one of the richest men in the world for doing nothing more than identifying investment opportunities and buying them…using a contrarian value investing style.

You can see why this is one method I keep ready to go at all times.

In the 30s, Benjamin Graham and David Dodd, both finance professors at Columbia University, are known as the father's of value investing.

The main philosophy is to find companies that are selling below their worth.

The value investor looks for a stock with strong fundamentals – book value, earnings, cash flow, dividends, etc. – that are selling for at a bargain price, when compared to what they are worth.

A good example of this is when Edward Lampert used his hedge fund to buy K-Mart out of bankruptcy because it had billions in real estate value alone and was selling for a fraction of the value.

So imagine buying a billion dollar company that is worth $50 billion for $850 million. There is great value there…even if all you did was sell off the assets.

The value investor wants to buy these stocks when they are being undervalued by the market, and buys them waiting for them to be correctly valued or in favor again.

Buy Value At A Bargain...Not Cheap Junk!

I don't want to give you guys the wrong impression here.

Value investing isn't buying stocks that are cheap just because they are cheap...it is buying them because they are high quality and shouldn't be selling so cheap.

Value investors do extensive research to make sure they are investing in stocks that are high quality. It is the only thing that they care about...buying stocks that shouldn't be cheap, but are...and watching the stocks increase in value realizing their true gain.

So if a company A was selling for $50 a share, but all of the sudden it is now $25 doesn't immediately make it a buy. There is more to it than that. All we know is that the company is less expensive now than it was before.

To be a real buy for a true value investor the company has to have strong fundamentals indicating that it is worth more than the current $25 per share selling price...value investors measure the current share price to it's intrinsic value...not the historic share price.

Greatest Champion

Warren Buffet as I said before is the most famous value investor.

Here's why:

- Share price of his holding company Berkshire Hathaway went from $12 per share in 196, to a current share price of $190,000

- The company consistently beats the S&P 500 every year Warren has had control of it every year
- Will wait for years for a great company to sell at a price that makes sense to him…classic value investing concepts.

What are you really buying?

One thing that value investors do when buying shares in a company is in how they think. They believe that when they buy shares into a company, they aren't just buying pieces of paper, but buying ownership into a company.

To a value investor money is made in investing and holding onto great companies. The money is made in investing…not trading.

Because they are looking for what a company is actually worth, they pay no attention to fluctuations in the stock price, and other stuff that is external that affects a company. They only care about what is going with that company itself.

Only factors that are inherent to the company matter to value investors.

Contradictions

Value Investors love contradictions. What contradictions are they most fond of?

Efficient Market Hypothesis otherwise known as EMH.

EMH says that prices are always reflecting all relevant information, so they are already showing the intrinsic worth of companies.

Value investors act on a principle that opposes that theory.

Value investors count on the EMH being true only in some theoretical fairytale. They look for times of inefficiency, when the market assigns an incorrect price to a stock, and then they pounce getting in on a great deal.

Another contradiction that value investors have is that they don't believe a high beta (wall street gibberish for volatility) means that a stock is a risky investment.

A company with an intrinsic value of $70 per share, but trading at $55 would be, based off just that quick calculation, an attractive investment to value investors. If the share price dropped to $40 per share, the company would experience an increase in beta, which conventionally represents an increase in risk.

However, the value investor still maintained that the intrinsic value was $70 per share, she would see the decline in price as an even better bargain. And the better the bargain, the lesser the risk.

High beta does not scare off value investors. Not as long as they are confident in their intrinsic valuation, an increase in downside volatility may be a good thing.

How do we find value stocks?

You can find value stocks on any trading index in the world. Value stocks are not limited to the US…no matter where you go if there is a stock market you can find a value stock.

Taking my above statement further value stocks can be found in any industry. Even technology…an industry my mentor Warren Buffet doesn't invest in at all…but there are some value plays once you do the work.

Although value stocks can be located anywhere, they are often located in industries that have recently fallen on hard times, or are currently facing market overreaction to a piece of news affecting the industry in the short term.

For example, the auto industry's cyclical nature allows for periods of undervaluation of companies such as Ford or GM…especially GM. Right now with what is going on with the company and all the recalls and bad press; if you believe it can bounce back than it could be a good value play.

I won't get into the particulars of how I feel about certain sectors and industry here.

WRONG!

I will speak my mind…I don't like the auto industry as an investment. They are too price competitive and the economics of the business don't really work for me.

A trade yes, but an investment no.

A good shopping list to find great opportunities is the new low list. Especially if you have done your homework and find that a company is great, but the stock is just temporarily broken.

On the flipside I like to invest in stocks that have recently hit a new high on the new high list. Not buying it at the high of course, but waiting for a pullback to pull the trigger.

There are a number of things that I look for in a stock as a value investment…or an investment period. That is for another book so let's keep moving forward.

There are many ways to find a value investment that I prefer over others and that is in another book, but the one thing I want to talk about here before I forget is the Margin of Safety.

So how can I best describe Margin of Safety?

Ready?

Imagine there is a viscous attack dog that is tied to a fence and a chain. You taunt the dog and know that it can only go 15 feet before it is stopped so you stand just outside that range.

The margin of safety would be to add an extra 5 feet or so just to make sure you are safe. Actually in this case maybe an extra 10-15+ feet cause I imagine the chain breaking.

(Why did I choose that example? Well I actually taunted a junkyard dog with friends when I was younger…very scary and stupid, but I was young and invincible.)

Margin of Safety works the same in value investing.

It's simply leaving room for error in your calculations of intrinsic value. A value investor may be pretty confident that a company has an intrinsic value of $100 per share. But just in case his or her calculations are a little too optimistic, he creates a margin of safety/error by using the $50 per share in their scenario analysis.

The investor may find that at $25 the company is still an attractive investment, or he may find that at $44, the company is not attractive enough.

If the stock's intrinsic value is lower than the investor estimated, the margin of safety would help prevent this investor from paying too much for the stock

Wrap It Up

Value investing is the more dry of the investing style. It is strict, rigid, and super disciplined way of investing.

But nothing is better than seeing you consistently beat the S&P 500 and even other money managers. We are a competitive bunch after all.

<u>Income Investing</u>

I want to say this is my favorite, but it isn't…just one of my key strategies to getting a ROI. (I'm a multi-strategy type of guy.)

The goal of income investing is to earn a consistent stream of income…not just capital appreciation, but income generation.

Most investors when they think of income investing think of bonds and other fixed-income securities. As much as I love bonds, why not go for income that you can get along with appreciation in your initial investment outside of yield.

Dividends: Where Can You Find Them?

Normally the only companies that give a dividend are older, more established businesses that aren't going to be growing at crazy high levels of growth anymore. These are companies that normally aren't in expanding industries…these are industries that are in their maturity (think utilities).

Because of these conditions, companies don't reinvest the earnings, but instead pay back all or most of those earnings back to the shareholders.

Like I said above the utility industry is famous for paying dividends. There are more, but that is the one where you would be hard pressed to find a company that isn't offering a dividend.

Yield, To Be or Not to Be

When you start investing for income the trick is to not focus on the dollar amounts that the company is offering you. Just like when investing in stocks, the share price means nothing…it's all about the multiple.

Well when investing for income it isn't about the dollar amount that the company is giving you. What's more important is the dividend yield.

How you calculate the dividend yield is easier than you may think. You just take the annual dividend amount and divide it by the share price. That's all there is to it.

So a company that is selling for $50 per share and has a annual dividend payout of
$10, has a dividend yield of 20%. Now that is very high, but you get the point. In this scenario the yield is 20% meaning that you are getting back a 20% return on your money from the dividend.

Like I said 20% is high, very rare, and dangerous. No company wants to offer a dividend that high, but it really is a case by case scenario. Typical is 6% and below. The S&P 500 typically offers a dividend of 2-3%.

Income investors need more than a measly 2-3% return. Most want a 5-6% yield. So if you take a typically invest in my fund of between $1 million minimum and sometimes as much $10 million at one time, could get from $50,000 - $600,000 a year.

That's why I love to keep this strategy in my back pocket ready when I need it.

So the principle is easy to understand…find great companies with consistent stable high dividends and receive a steady stream of income. Most companies pay their dividends every quarter (3 months).

You also want to look at the dividend policy of any company you are thinking of investing in…especially if you're only investing for the income stream. Income investors have to decide if the dividend is safe and the company can continue to pay it out.

There are a few things to be on the lookout for. Say a company increases its' dividend from 1% to 6%...that is a hefty hike. Especially when they say they are going to be doing it over a short period of time (thinking a year or two).

A move like that could be too optimistic and unsustainable. The companies that have been paying a dividend for years (10-50+ years), and also have been increasing their dividend over time will most likely continue to do so.

Added bonus is that when you reinvest your dividends and you invest in a solid company you can increase your annual rate of return exponentially.

All That Glitters Ain't Gold

Dividends aren't everything though. I don't want you to just buy a stock that has a high yield...that isn't smart. You should be investing in solid companies with solid returns, solid financials, and solid fundamentals.

I know you want to go out and find a stock screener and just look for all the high yielders and go crazy.

WAIT!!!

Imagine a company offering a 20% dividend yield, but if you just looked at their balance sheet you see that they can't even pay their bills for the next year and will have to file for bankruptcy. Do you really think a company like that can afford to pay you anything?

So remember that what you are doing is buying stocks of companies. So you want to make sure that what you invest in is viable, and it makes sense. This way you know for sure the dividend is likely to last.

Also please talk to your tax professionals…dividends are taxable income and depending on where you live can even be more than capital gains tax. So just look out for that.

Must-Own Date

I almost forgot something important.

When looking to buy a stock for it's dividend there is a date that you must buy to be eligible for the dividend.

They will mention a lot of dates as it pertains to the dividend, such as date of record, ex-dividend date, etc. But what you want to do is buy it the day before the stock goes ex-dividend.

The ex-dividend date is easy to find…so just look at that date and make sure you own the stock a day before that date and you will be fine.

Here's an example:

Let's say XYZ Corp., which is trading at $10 a share, declares a regular quarterly dividend today of 10 cents a share for a 4% yield. The dividend is payable to shareholders of record (meaning those who own the stock) on Thursday, Dec. 13.

Looking at the calendar, we can determine that the ex-date will be Tuesday, the 11th and the must-own date will be Monday, the 10th. So as long as you own the stock by close of trading on Monday, the 10th you will receive the dividend.

<u>Growth Investing</u>

Wall Street is all about growth. Sometimes I believe the mantra is growth at all cost. So because most of Wall Street is obsessed with growth, growth investing techniques can yield ridiculous results for investors.

But before you monkey see, monkey do wait until you learn more about this method of making money. One thing is that more investors loose money chasing stock prices than most any other strategy.

Value vs. Growth: Both Go In and One Comes Out

If value investing is all about taking your time, being sensible, and being careful, than growth investing is going 90 miles per hour in a residential area. Yes, they are that opposite to each other.

Value investors look at a company at what it is doing now…it looks for a company trading for less than it's intrinsic value.

Growth investors are all about the future. They are all about the possibilities, hopes, and dreams of what a company could become. Growth investors look for companies that are trading at higher than their intrinsic value. They do this because they believe that the intrinsic value of the company is growing as fast as the stock price, so it warrants them buying now.

Growth stocks are growing faster than any other stocks. Of course, there are many ways to classify a growth stock. You have high growth, consistent growers, and my favorite slow growers…though we are only talking about high growth stocks here.

The only companies that tend to be high growth stocks are younger companies. Companies beginning to catch heat on Wall Street.

Growth investors believe that the rapid growing in revenues (earnings growth depends on the industry…Amazon.com is a high growth stock and never turned a profit for years until recently.) will increase the stock price of the company.

Growth stocks are typically found in industries that have new technologies attached to them. You will never find a high growth stock in a utility company…just nothing there to light a spark. But technology sees the most growth…the next is retail.

Growth stocks don't pay dividends. The only way for a growth investor to realize any profit is through capital gains (selling the stock for a higher price than they paid for it).

No Magic Pill

Growth investors care about a company's future value, and their future growth potential. Because of this…there is no set formula for determining this potential. All methods of determining growth stocks (all methods of stock picking) are up to the individual to decide…very subjective.

Growth investors use certain criteria to determining if a stock meets their criteria. Not only do they have to take each company specific situation into consideration, but also the industry, and past performance, and the economy.

So though there are no magic formulas or magic pill to picking great growth stocks, growth investors can and do develop guidelines and a set list of criteria when picking stocks to make sure they win.

NAIC

The NAIC (National Association of Investors Corporation) is one of the best and most well-known organizations teaching and using growth investing.

It is, as it says on its website, "one big investment club" whose goal is to teach investors how to invest wisely. The NAIC has developed some basic "universal" guidelines for finding possible growth companies.

Here's a look at some of the questions the NAIC suggests you should ask when considering stocks, as taken from my friends at www.investopedia.com:

1. Strong Historical Earnings Growth?
The first question a growth investor should ask is whether the company, based on annual revenue, has been growing in the past. Below are rough guidelines for the rate of EPS growth an investor should look for in companies of differing sizes, which would indicate their growth investing potential:

Company Size	Minimum Growth in Last 5 Years
> $4B	5%
> $400M >$4B	7%
< $400M	12%

Although the NAIC suggests that companies display this type of EPS growth in at least the last five years, a 10-year period of this growth is even more attractive. The basic idea is that if a company has displayed good growth (as defined by the above chart) over the last five- or 10-year period, it is likely to continue doing so in the next five to 10 years.

2. Strong Forward Earnings Growth?
The second criterion set out by the NAIC is a projected five-year growth rate of at least 10-12%, although 15% or more is ideal. These projections are made by analysts, the company or other credible sources.

The big problem with forward estimates is that they are estimates. When a growth investor sees an ideal growth projection, he or she, before trusting this projection, must evaluate its credibility. This requires knowledge of the typical growth rates for different sizes of companies. For example, an established large cap will not be able to grow as quickly as a younger small-cap tech company. Also, when evaluating analyst consensus estimates, an investor should learn about the company's industry - specifically, what its prospects are and what stage of growth it is at.

3. Is Management Controlling Costs and Revenues?
The third guideline set out by the NAIC focuses specifically on pre-tax profit margins. There are many examples of companies with astounding growth in sales but less than outstanding gains in earnings. High annual revenue growth is good, but if EPS has not increased proportionately, it's likely due to a decrease in profit margin.

By comparing a company's present profit margins to its past margins and its competition's profit margins, a growth investor is able to gauge accurately whether or not management is controlling costs and revenues and maintaining margins. A good rule of thumb is that if company exceeds its previous five-year average of pre-tax profit margins as well as those of its industry, the company may be a good growth candidate.

4. Can Management Operate the Business Efficiently?
Efficiency can be quantified by using return on equity (ROE). Efficient use of assets should be reflected in a stable or increasing ROE. Again, analysis of this metric should be relative: a company's present ROE is best compared to the five-year average ROE of the company and the industry.

5. Can the Stock Price Double in Five Years?
If a stock cannot realistically double in five years, it's probably not a growth stock. That's the general consensus. This may seem like an overly high, unrealistic standard, but remember that with a growth rate of 10%, a stock's price would double in seven years. So the rate

growth investors are seeking is 15% per annum, which yields a doubling in price in five years.

An Example

Now that we've outlined the NAIC's basic criteria for evaluating growth stocks, let's demonstrate how these criteria are used to analyze a company, using Microsoft's 2003 figures. For the sake of this demonstration, we'll discuss these numbers as though they were Microsoft's most current figures (that is, "today's figures").

1. Five-Year Earnings Figures

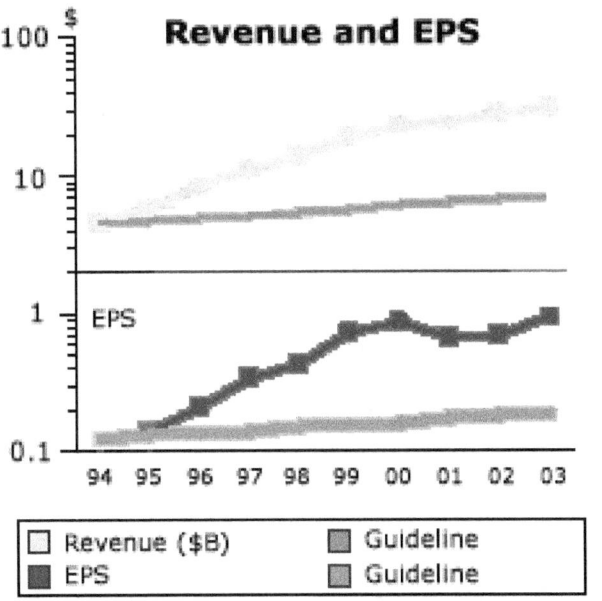

- Five-year average annual sales growth is 15.94%.
- Five-year average annual EPS growth is 10.91%.

Both of these are strong figures. The annual EPS growth is well above the 5% standard the NAIC sets out for firms of Microsoft's size.

2. Strong Projected Earnings Growth

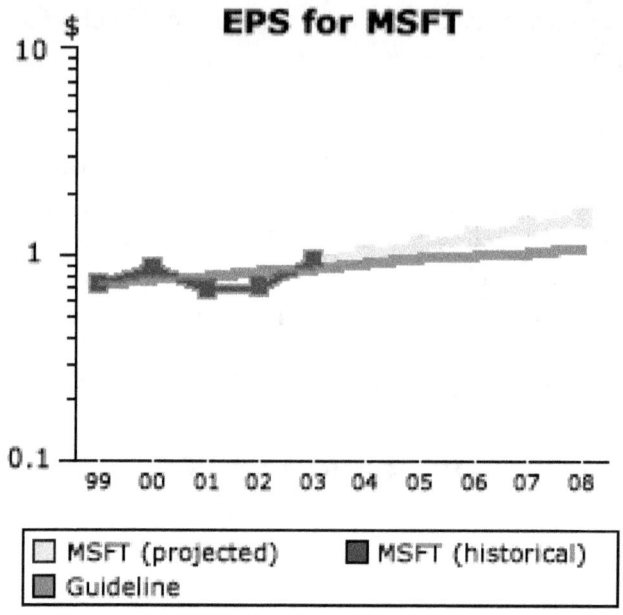

EPS for MSFT

Legend:
- MSFT (projected)
- MSFT (historical)
- Guideline

• Five-year projected average annual earnings growth is 11.03%.

The projected growth figures are strong, but not exceptional.

3. Costs and Revenue Control

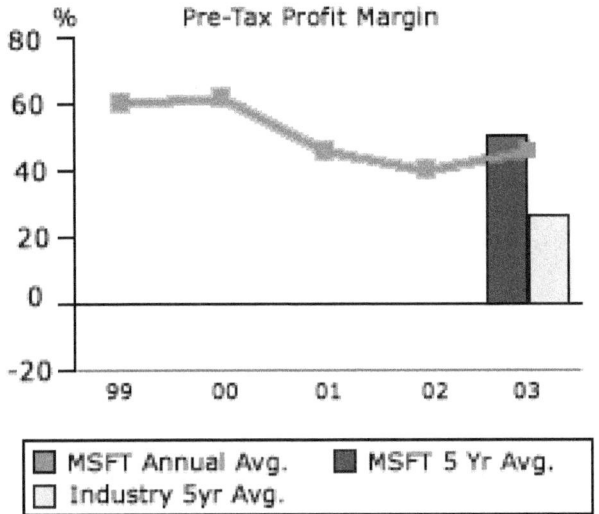

- Pre-tax margin in most recent fiscal year is 45.80%.
- Five-year average fiscal pre-tax margin is 50.88%.
- Industry\'s five-year average pre-tax margin is 26.7%.

There are two ways to look at this. The trend is down 5.08% (50.88% - 45.80%) from the five-year average, which is negative. But notice that the industry's average margin is only 26.7%. So even though Microsoft's margins have dropped, they're still a great deal higher than those of its industry.

4. ROE

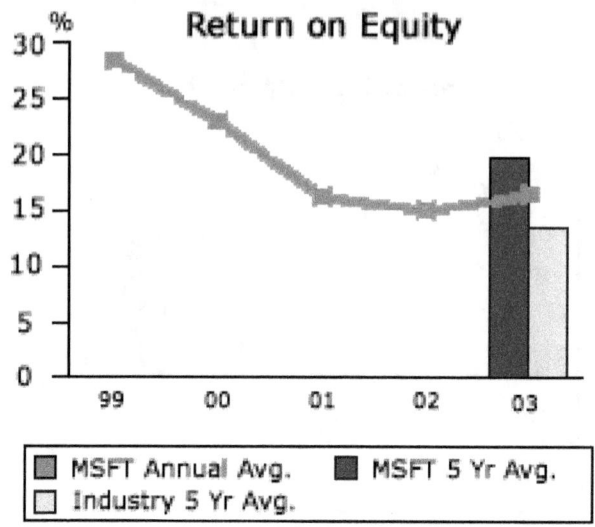

- Most recent fiscal year-end is ROE 16.40%.
- Five-year average ROE is 19.80%.
- Industry average five-year ROE is 13.60%.

Again, it's a point of concern that the ROE figure is a little lower than the five-year average. However, like Microsoft's profit margin, the ROE is not drastically reduced - it's only down a few points and still well above the industry average.

5. Potential to Double in Five Years

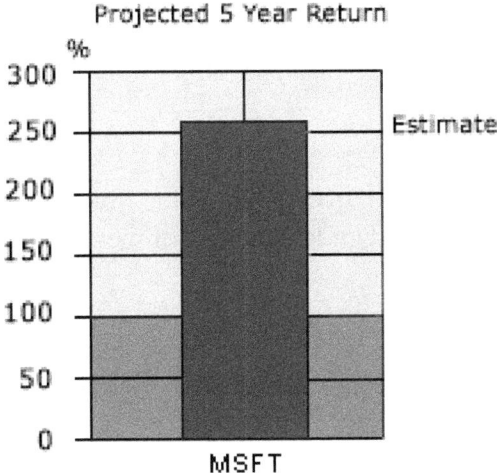

• Stock is projected to appreciate by 254.7%.

The average analyst projections for Microsoft suggest that in five years the stock will not merely double in value, but it'll be worth 254.7% its current value

Last Thing

Bottom line growth investors are concerned with growth above all else. The point behind growth investing is to look for companies that keep reinvesting into themselves to produce new products and technology.

Even though the stocks is expensive using the current evaluations growth investors believe that if the top and bottom lines are growing at an alarming rate they are assured that the investment pays off in the long run.

<u>GARP</u>

We've already talked about growth and value investing. If you think that you have a pretty good understanding of these styles than you are ready.

Think of GARP as the love child of value and growth. GARP is otherwise known as growth at a reasonable price.

Who are you?

GARP is a strategy that combines both growth principles and value principles. It looks for companies that are undervalued, but have growth potential. The key is looking right in between both disciplines.

Some believe that GARP investors just accept any stock…that there isn't a foundation or leg for them to stand on. This is false. Like the other methodologies those who practice GARP look for certain stocks that fit a certain criteria.

I've even heard that GARP investors just have a portfolio full of value and growth stocks. Now I am a big believer in diversification, and that means not only in the sector the stocks belong to, but also the type of stock (value, income, growth).

So don't think that GARPers will just choose 20 stocks and make ½ value, and the other ½ growth. That isn't the case.

One of the greatest known GARP investors is Peter Lynch. He has had a 29% annual average return on his portfolio. This is the power of using GARP…incorporating growth and value techniques.

Characteristics

GARP investors are concerned with the growth outlook of a company. They like to see that a company has been hitting their earnings numbers (actually beating the earning estimates would be better), and has positive earnings projections for the following and future years.

GARP and growth investors differ in that GARPers don't want a company that is growing 25-50%. The reason is simple…companies growing that fast are too risky. The minute they hit disappointing numbers (and it does happen to every single one of them sooner or later) they take a serious hit. Money pours out of them faster than you can think.

A safer growth rate is more in the 10-20% range for those who practice GARP investors.

GARP investors want a high ROE. Just like growth investors. A high ROE relative to the industry average is a key indicator to these investors.

Another area where growth investors and GARP investors differ is in the area of PROFITS!!!! Growth investors are concerned with an increase in revenues. GARP investors are not only focused on top line growth, but also bottom line growth. They want to see a company with healthy profits.

GARP investors take advantage of the fact that they have a number of different criteria to make decisions based on what will make a company grow faster than the rest. So just like growth investing you must take the individual company into consideration, economy as a whole, and the story.

Not just a high growth number…

It's the same thing I said about the income investors and a super high dividend yield. All that glitters ain't gold.

GARP investors look for a P/E ratio that is higher what a value investor would be comfortable with, but also less than what a pure growth investor would look for. Growth investors could look for a P/E as high as 50…for GARP investors that number is unacceptable because it means they are paying too much for the company.

Like the value investor, GARP investors like to see a low price-to-book ratio (P/B). A low P/E and a low P/B are where the GARP investors and the value investors are similar.

PEG

GARP investors look at the PEG ratio as the holy grail. It gives an indication of a stock's growth potential and it's value.

From what I see GARP investors like a PEG ratio of at least .5-1.

Why?

A PEG of less than one means that the stock is cheaper than it should be considering its growth. So when a GARPer sees a PEG of less than 1, that is a screaming signal that the stock at least warrants a deeper look.

GARP in Action

So because GARP investors are right down the middle when it comes to growth and value investing methods they tend to do in the middle type of numbers.

Let me explain…

When we are in a bull market growth investors are the undecided winners hands down. No one can compete with a growth investor in their market…the bull market is the growth market. The downside is that what comes up, do come down.

So when the bull turns into a bear growth investors get hurt…and get hurt bad. Sometimes returning all of the gains they made. So GARPers suffer less in this scenario than pure growth investors.

So though a growth investor does great in a bull market; a value investor does great in a bear market; the GARPer will not do as great as its extreme parents, but it will be the most consistent and predictable earner.

Conclusion

Now I know I probably made GARP sound like it's the perfect investment strategy to follow. After all why not get the best of both worlds, and if Peter Lynch followed it than it can't be all bad…right?

But you have to be a true master of value and growth investing. The reason why is because you cannot be a true GARP investor if you haven't gotten down the basics of value and growth investor.

Maybe that's why Peter Lynch did as great as he did, and is in the Investors Hall of Fame.

CAN SLIM

In my other book, World's Greatest Investors, I talked about the great investor William O'Neil. He's the founder of Investor's Business Daily, and when you read his book "How to Make Money in Stocks" (yes I am referring other books…I am all about spreading the wealth and knowledge.)

O'Neil is the creator of CAN SLIM; its a way of purchasing, screening, and selling common stock.

So the thing about CAN SLIM is that it is actually a very successful way to pick stocks, because it focuses not only the tangibles like earnings, but also the intangibles. So you can look at most companies and apply the CAN SLIM criteria and increased dramatically in price.

If you haven't guessed by now, CAN SLIM is an acronym that we will break down for you right now.

C = Current Earnings

You want to choose a stock whose earnings per share (EPS) has grown on a yearly basis. You want to look at the current EPS for that current quarter. So if I am looking at a company at the end of year quarter, I need to look at the past year's end of year quarter to compare.

Which when you think about it makes sense. If I am analyzing a retail stock like Gap, I know retail stocks make the most of their money during the last quarter of the year, so I need to compare the previous year's same quarter and see how they compare.

So we are looking for quarter after quarter growth. Something in the high growth stock range of over 20% would be ideal…but again you need to take into consideration your goals and tolerance level to risk.

You want to make sure that the earnings are high quality too. You don't want to invest in a stock that has dying or even false earnings. What can make earnings false is management manipulating numbers. That is why you want to measure the EPS versus the income statement and the operating ratios.

A = Annual Earnings

In this section of CAN SLIM we want to see good annual EPS growth over the past 5 years.

From talking to CAN SLIM investors they seem very much like my value investor friends in that they believe when they are buying stock they are actually buying ownership in a company.

O'Neil says that you should be investing in a company with 25-50% annual EPS growth range. No one wants to buy into a business where there is no growth.

O'Neil says that Wal-Mart is an example of a company whose strong annual growth preceded a large run-up in share price. Between 1977 and 1990, Wal-Mart displayed an average annual earnings growth of 43%.

N = New

The third criterion for a good company is it has recently undergone a change (which is often key for a company to become successful). O'Neil doesn't care whether it is a new management team, a new product, a new market, or a new high in stock price.

O'Neil found that 95% of the companies he studied had experienced something new.

McDonald's is the reigning king of something new…they are always doing promotions and introducing something new to spark interest and business. With the introduction of its new fast food franchises, it grew over 1100% in four years from 1967 to 1971!

That is just one example of companies that, through doing or acquiring something new, achieved great things and rewarded their shareholders along the way.

Another example of a company that is all about new and innovation is Disney. They are always doing something to spark business and work at doing some big and interesting.

Another area that is new that most investors run from is new price highs. Investors fear that a company that has recently hit a new high will fall from that level.

O'Neil uses very detailed and compelling historical data to show that stocks that have just reached new highs often continue on an upward trend to even higher levels.

Another person who uses the new high technique (besides me) is my mentor Jim Cramer. You can learn a lot from watching is show Mad Money.

S = Supply and Demand

I know what you're probably thinking. You remember this from economics and think you can just skip this section.

WRONG!!!!!

Even if you think you know, just take the 1-minute it will take to read this. Don't skimp on the fundamentals. After all supply and demand govern all market activities. I think you should give it, it's due.

So this is all about the shares a company has outstanding (not owned by anyone and offered to the public and available for anyone to buy). It says that a smaller company with less shares outstanding can increase in price faster than its equivalent that has many, many times more the shares outstanding.

Why?

Well because small cap stocks require little demand, especially when compared to large cap stocks to cause a huge run up in the price.

O'Neil explains this concept a little further.

According to O'Neil the lack of liquidity of large institutional investors restricts them to buying only large-cap, blue chip companies, leaving these large investors at a serious disadvantage that small individual investors can capitalize on.

These huge mammoths cannot buy a small cap stock and get enough stock to make a difference in their performance.

Because of supply and demand, the large transactions that institutional investors make can inadvertently affect share price, especially if the stock's market capitalization is smaller.

Now because individual investors invest smaller amounts than their ginormous siblings, they can get in or out of a smaller company without pushing share price in an unfavorable direction.

O'Neil found that 95% of the companies displaying the largest gains in share price had fewer than 25 million shares outstanding when the gains were realized

L = Leader or Laggard

BEST OF BREED.

Go for the best of breed. I cannot think of a reason why you wouldn't go for the best of breed. Actually yes I can…maybe if you are going for a takeover target, or maybe a speculative stock than you don't want to go the best of breed route.

No matter what industry you are researching there will always be a leader of the pack. Now sometimes it is harder to tell if the competition is really fierce.

There is a metric called the "Relative Price Strength."

The relative price strength of a stock can range from 1 to 99. A rank of 75 means the company, over a given period of time, has outperformed 75% of the stocks in its market group.

CAN SLIM investors require a stock to have a relative price strength of at least 70.

O'Neil states that stocks with relative price strength in the 80–90 range are more likely to be the major gainers.

Cheap stocks are cheap for a reason. Do not go for the cheap alternative, because it is cheap. That makes no sense. Best of breed stocks are more expensive than others in their industry, because they deserve to be.

Go for quality.

I = Institutional Sponsorship

What is meant by institutional sponsorships is that the huge mutual funds, hedge funds, pension funds, other businesses are investing in the company. This is a sign that the company is doing something right.

If no one is invested in the business than it is a sign that none of the pros think the stock is worthwhile…something to think about.

Think what happens when Warren Buffet blesses a stock with buying it. Everyone jumps in.

Institutional sponsorship can be that important.

But be careful. When we had that bad recession starting in 2008 it was because hedge funds were selling their shares in companies in droves. That is why companies saw their share prices plummet. When a hedge fund and mutual fund own millions and millions of shares in a company and dump it all out onto the market bad things happen.

A $100 stock can quickly go down to a single digit stock. Think of Citibank, AIG, and others.

So the best thing to do is to know who the institutions are. Who are your fellow shareholders…why?

Cause someone like Warren Buffett is known for staying in the long run and staying in a company for decades. So you know he is in it, to win it.

Someone who is more of a trader will dump out at the first sign of bad news.

M = Market Direction

Are we in a bear or bull market?

Why did you choose what you chose?

Are you sure?

What are the trends?

I am not promoting being a market timer, and neither is O'Neil by the way, you should at least know where we are in the marketplace and where the economy is going.

Why?

Because ultimately stock picking is about deciding not where a stock has been, but where it is going.

CAN SLIM argues that the best way to keep track of market conditions is to watch the daily volumes and movements of the markets. This component of CAN SLIM may require the use of some technical analysis (we'll get to technical analysis later) tools.

Those tools are designed to help investors/traders discern trends, and make their decisions.

Here's a recap of the seven CAN SLIM criteria as presented by O'Neil:

1. **C = Current quarterly earnings per share** - Earnings must be up at least 18-20% from the previous year.
2. **A = Annual earnings per share** – These figures should show meaningful growth for the last five years. CAN SLIM investors like to see 25-50% growth in this area.
3. **N = New things** - Buy companies with new products, new management, or significant new changes in industry conditions. Most importantly, buy stocks when they start to hit new price highs. Forget cheap stocks; they are that way for a reason.
4. **S = Shares outstanding** - This should be a small and reasonable number. CAN SLIM investors are not looking for older companies with a large capitalization. Small to Mid cap stocks are ideal.
5. **L = Leaders** – BUY BEST OF BREED!!!!! Leave the rest for the fools.
6. **I = Institutional sponsorship** - Buy stocks with at least a few institutional sponsors who have better-than-average recent performance records…think Warren Buffet.
7. **M = General market** - The market will determine whether you win or lose, so learn how to discern the market's overall current direction, and interpret the general market indexes

(price and volume changes) and action of the individual market leaders.

CAN SLIM is great because it provides solid guidelines, keeping subjectivity to a minimum. It's what most investors want…tell me what to do to make money and I'll do it.

The best thing is that it incorporates tactics from virtually all of the major investment strategies. Think of it as a combination of value, growth, fundamental, and even the mysterious stepchild technical analysis.

If you want more information on this investing style please read O'Neil's book, "How to Make Money in Stocks". I recommend reading the book to fully understand the underlying concepts of CAN SLIM.

I use CAN SLIM along with the other styles to make my own decisions. O'Neil's book is a staple in my library.

Dogs of the Dow

This is the only other strategy that I'll be talking about, that takes into account the dividend yield.

This strategy comes from Michael Higgins, in his book "Beating the Dow," Dogs of the Dow wins major points with investors because of it's simplicity. Put simply the Dogs of the Dow strategy is to simply find the top 10 of the 30 stocks in the DJIA with the highest dividend.

All the investor has to do is shuffle the DJIA stocks so that he always has the top 10 with the highest dividend yields.

How easy is that?

So about 3-4 times a year an investor would need to change their entire portfolio. Why? Because the stocks being changed have either fallen in their yield, thus not meeting the criteria of the top 10 of the 30…or the stock has been rejected from the DJIA all together.

It Can't Really Be That Easy…Is It?

Yes it is.

This strategy really is as simple as it sounds.

At the end of every year, you reassess the 30 components of the DJIA, determining which ones have the highest dividend yield. Than either you or your broker makes the change.

Hold onto these 10 stocks for one calendar year. When the new year starts, you just rinse and repeat. This is a long-term strategy…not a particularly sexy one, but effective.

It requires a long period to see results. There have been a few years in which the Dow has outperformed the Dogs, so it is the long-term averages that proponents of the strategy rely on.

Not my favorite strategy, but I am trying not to be overly biased...I am about making money and showing you how to make money. Since investors make money this way, here it is.

Foundations

Like contrarian value investors the gist of this investment style is the out-of-favor stocks in the DJIA, are still good companies...because they are still included in the DJIA.

The premise is that if the companies weren't worthy they would be dropped from the exchange.

So this investment philosophy is to basically buy these out of favor stocks, with high dividend yields, until the market realizes the mistake, and than gives them a higher price. Once the stocks receive a higher price the yield goes down, sparking the signal to change up your portfolio.

You change them to the now new out of favor stocks that will have the highest dividend yield.

Companies in the Dow historically have been very stable companies that can weather any market decline with their solid balance sheets and strong fundamentals.

Did you know that there is a committee continuously tinkering with the DJIA's list of stocks? That to me is reassuring cause you have professionals who always make sure that the DJIA is made up of good, solid companies.

Numbers Don't Lie

Besides this strategy being very simple to implement and understand it performs as well.

But there is one thing about it…the Dogs of the Dow strategy is to beat the stocks in the DJIA…not the benchmark Wall Street uses on a consistent basis. The S&P 500 is the benchmark to beat, but this strategy doesn't take into account this benchmark. It measures against the DJIA.

So with that being said, this strategy does beat the DJIA average returns by as much as 14.3% annually, where the DJIA would return an average of 11%.

Less Than Bulletproof

This should come to no surprise.

All the other strategies I've talked about I made it a point to say that you shouldn't put blind faith in any one strategy, because no one wins 100% of the time with any of these strategies.

Dogs of the Dow is no exception.

So you can use this strategy and if history repeats itself you will continue to beat the DJIA by 3% every year…if history repeats itself.

Side note: Since you are investing for yield, make sure you reinvest those dividends, cause that helps with the returns you generate!!!

Technical Analysis

So far in this book I've talked about many ways to pick stocks. The trick though is that they are all based on fundamental analysis.

Meaning that you are digging into the companies themselves, and making sure that they fit a certain criteria. In those previous styles you would care about the annual reports, the quarterly reports, EPS, ratios, income statements, cash flow statements, balance sheets, etc. to make your buying decisions.

Technical analysis is the ying to fundamental analysis' yang.

Technical analysts, or technicians as they are called in the biz, select stocks by analyzing statistics generated by past market activity…prices and volumes.

Technical analysts look at the past charts of prices and different indicators to make inferences about the future movement of a stock's price…that is why they are also called chartist.

Technical Analysis Primer

While talking to technicians, one book that came up again and again was "Charting Made Easy," by John Murphy who many revere as a guru of technical analysis.

Here is how he explains this philosophy:

"Chart analysis (also called technical analysis) is the study of market action, using price charts, to forecast future price direction. The cornerstone of the technical philosophy is the belief that all factors that influence market price - fundamental information, political events, natural disasters, and psychological factors - are quickly discounted in market activity. In other words, the impact of

these external factors will quickly show up in some form of price movement, either up or down."

Technical analysis has some assumptions already built into it. Here are some of the assumptions technicians adopt:

1. Prices move in predictable trends or patterns
2. All information on a stock are already built into the stock. It's the old EMH (efficient market hypothesis) all over again…
3. History repeats itself, making money all about again…recognizing patterns and trends in the market.

We Don't Give Two Nickels About The Rest Of It

When talking to some of my friends who are traders (pure technical traders that is) you should hear our conversations.

They don't care about anything that I care about.

Don't tell them anything about any management, business model, competition, P/E ratio, cash flow, etc.

They are concerned with the trends and patterns presented to them day to day.

The things that matter are past data, and charts and indicators. The awesome thing is they often make a lot of money trading companies they know almost nothing about.

Sprinters vs. Marathoners

This should be easy to understand. If fundamental investors are more long-term in their view, than technical traders are short term.

To a chartist long term is till end of the trading session…if that long.

Technical analysts are very active in their trades. They hold positions for short periods in order to capitalize on changes in price, whether up or down.

A technical analyst may go short or long on a stock, depending on what direction the data is saying the price will move.

I have friends that make about 400 trades in a single day. It is a full time job…not for the faint of heart…only true pros and the committed should attempt this.

Now with the advent of these high frequency trading methods, pennies are being traded on and yes even on that fortunes are being made.

If a stock does not perform the way a technician thought it would, he or she wastes little time deciding whether to exit his or her position. They just act…most using stop-loss orders to lessen losses.

On the other hand, a value investor must have a lot of patience and wait for the market to correct its undervaluation of a company. The technician doesn't have to play by the same rules. She must possess a great deal of trading agility and know how to get in and out of positions with speed.

Technical Analysis Concepts

Technicians have a very full toolbox of ways to buy and sell stocks.

They literally have hundreds of indicators and chart patterns to use for picking stocks.

It is important to note that no one indicator or chart pattern is infallible or absolute; the technician must interpret indicators and patterns, and this process is more subjective than formulaic.

Let's review one of the concepts that technicians adhere to.

Support and Resistance

One of the most important concepts in technical analysis are support and resistance.

These are the levels at which technicians expect a stock to start increasing after a decline (support), or to begin decreasing after an increase (resistance).

Trades are generally entered around these important levels because they indicate the way in which a stock will bounce. Enter into a long position if you feel a support level has been hit, or enter into a short position if you feel a resistance level has been hit.

Here is an illustration of where technicians might set support and resistance levels:

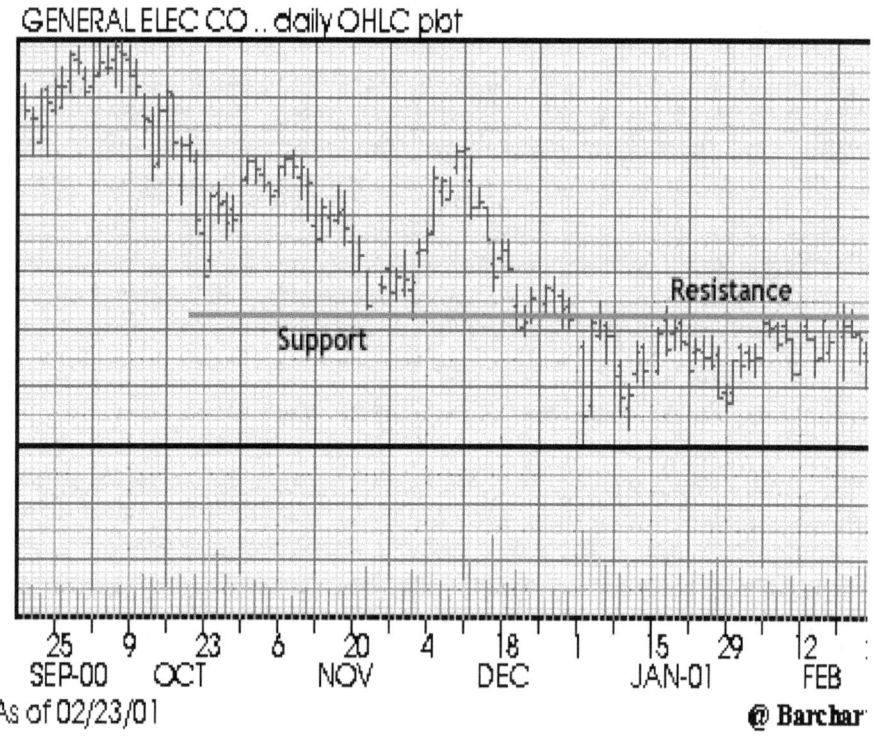

Now I want to show you a couple of the most popular chart patterns that technicians use. This isn't even the tip of the iceberg when it comes to charts. I could write a whole book on just the different charts and what they could mean. (Actually many have)

Cup and Handle

This is a bullish pattern that looks like a pot with a handle.

The stock price is expected to break out at the end of the handle, so by buying here, investors are able to make a lot of money. Technicians' love this pattern cause t is very easy to see.

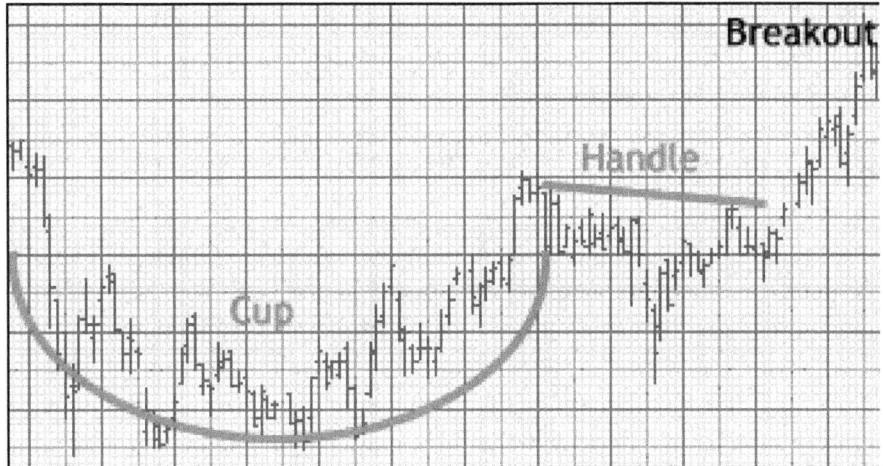

Head and Shoulders

This pattern resembles a head with two shoulders. Not as easy to see as the cup and handle. Technicians usually consider this a bearish pattern.

Below is an example of this particular chart pattern:

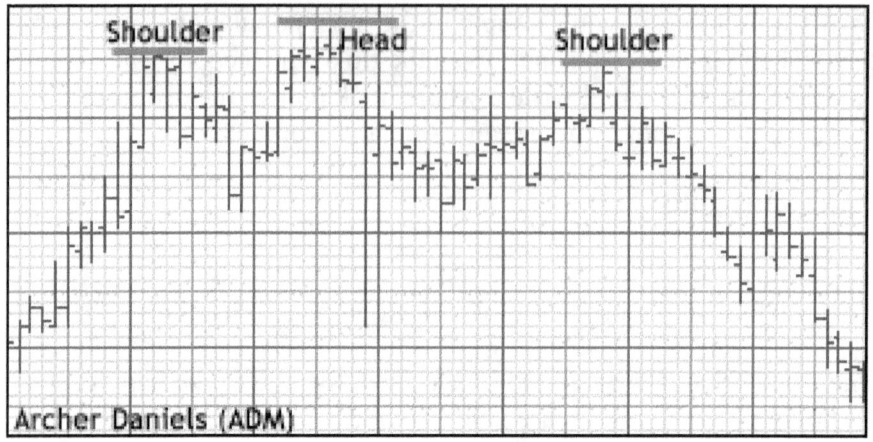

Archer Daniels (ADM)

I wanted to stop here cause I felt myself going out of control adding all these patterns and the corresponding charts to them. But than I decided I will do that in a future book that I will write on technical analysis for the fundamentalist.

Conclusion

Technical analysis is unlike any other stock-picking strategy. It has its own set of concepts, and it relies on a completely different set of criteria than any other strategy that uses fundamental analysis.

Don't mistake that because technicians take less information when compared to other strategies that it is easy. Regardless of its super analytical approach, mastering technical analysis requires discipline and savvy, just like any other strategy.

I do not pretend to be a technician. To be honest it isn't my strong suit, but as a money manager, I need to know all the tools at my disposal.

Also, a lot of the big hedge funds and mutual funds make decisions based off of technical analysis, so it is smart of me to know how they think to use it to make me and my clients more money.

So for that reason it wouldn't hurt to know something about this stock picking strategy as well.

I believe it is worthwhile. Not just because I employ both short and long-term strategies, but because I want you to know all you can so you can decide which strategy fits you best.

__Conclusion__

So here we are at the end...

My advice to you if you are concerned at where to start is to decide first what are your goals.

Are you in this for quick money?

Are you looking for an investment to buy and hold?

Your goals and your tolerance for risk will dictate which strategy you follow.

Though I am more of a fundamental guy, doesn't mean I don't take advantage of short-term trends and profits. That's me…what is right for you is right for you.

Maybe in your young age, you can trade more and invest less, and as you get older, you can invest more, and trade very little. Like I said…it depends on you.

Warren Buffet has been following his strategy for decades and is the World's Richest Investor. His counter part George Soros is more of a short-term trader, and is also a multi-billionaire in his own right.

So you have to decide what is right for you.

Bonus Chapter

Bottoms Up Investing

In bottoms up investing you put your focus first and foremost on the company. The economy and market cycles aren't taken into consideration until the company has been thoroughly analyzed.

So with someone who is following this theory of investing what you want to do is find a company...say Walmart and do all your analysis and than decided what it takes to make this business grow and expand.

So you look at Walmart and than decide what type of economy and market will cause Walmart to make more money, thus causing an increase in share price.

Top Down Investing

Top down investing is obviously the opposite of bottoms up investing.

In the top down investing world you look at what is going on in the world of economics to make your decisions. You look at the macro and micro economic trends, and than decide what type of companies do best or worse in that economy.

For example, if you see there is a hike in interest rates, you will know that bank stocks will go down, but consumer good product companies like Procter and Gamble, Johnson and Johnson, and Coca-Cola will go up during this time.

Hedge Fund Strategies

The following strategies are from the great people over at www.hedgeco.net. I was writing them down, and see that they did such a good job, why not tap into that knowledge.

Aggressive Growth:
Invests in equities expected to experience acceleration in growth of earnings per share. Generally high P/E ratios, low or no dividends; often smaller and micro cap stocks which are expected to experience rapid growth. Includes sector specialist funds such as technology, banking, or biotechnology. Hedges by shorting equities where earnings disappointment is expected or by shorting stock indexes. Tends to be "long-biased."
Expected Volatility: High

Distressed Securities
Buys equity, debt, or trade claims at deep discounts of companies in or facing bankruptcy or reorganization. Profits from the market's lack of understanding of the true value of the deeply discounted securities and because the majority of institutional investors cannot own below investment grade securities. (This selling pressure creates the deep discount.) Results generally not dependent on the direction of the markets.
Expected Volatility: Low – Moderate

Emerging Markets:
Invests in equity or debt of emerging (less mature) markets that tend to have higher inflation and volatile growth. Short selling is not permitted in many emerging markets, and, therefore, effective hedging is often not available, although Brady debt can be partially hedged via U.S. Treasury futures and currency markets.
Expected Volatility: Very High

Funds of Hedge Funds:
Mix and match hedge funds and other pooled investment vehicles. This blending of different strategies and asset classes aims to provide a more stable long-term investment return than any of the individual funds. Returns, risk, and volatility can be controlled by the mix of underlying strategies and funds. Capital preservation is generally an important consideration. Volatility depends on the mix and ratio of

strategies employed.
Expected Volatility: Low – Moderate – High

Income:

Invests with primary focus on yield or current income rather than solely on capital gains. May utilize leverage to buy bonds and sometimes fixed income derivatives in order to profit from principal appreciation and interest income.
Expected Volatility: Low

Macro:

Aims to profit from changes in global economies, typically brought about by shifts in government policy that impact interest rates, in turn affecting currency, stock, and bond markets. Participates in all major markets — equities, bonds, currencies and commodities — though not always at the same time. Uses leverage and derivatives to accentuate the impact of market moves. Utilizes hedging, but the leveraged directional investments tend to make the largest impact on performance.
Expected Volatility: Very High

Market Neutral – Arbitrage:

Attempts to hedge out most market risk by taking offsetting positions, often in different securities of the same issuer. For example, can be long convertible bonds and short the underlying issuers equity. May also use futures to hedge out interest rate risk. Focuses on obtaining returns with low or no correlation to both the equity and bond markets. These relative value strategies include fixed income arbitrage, mortgage backed securities, capital structure arbitrage, and closed-end fund arbitrage.
Expected Volatility: Low

Market Neutral – Securities Hedging:

Invests equally in long and short equity portfolios generally in the same sectors of the market. Market risk is greatly reduced, but effective stock analysis and stock picking is essential to obtaining meaningful results. Leverage may be used to enhance returns. Usually low or no correlation to the market. Sometimes uses market index futures to hedge out systematic (market) risk. Relative

benchmark index usually T-bills.
Expected Volatility: Low

Market Timing:
Allocates assets among different asset classes depending on the manager's view of the economic or market outlook. Portfolio emphasis may swing widely between asset classes. Unpredictability of market movements and the difficulty of timing entry and exit from markets add to the volatility of this strategy.
Expected Volatility: High

Opportunistic:
Investment theme changes from strategy to strategy as opportunities arise to profit from events such as IPOs, sudden price changes often caused by an interim earnings disappointment, hostile bids, and other event-driven opportunities. May utilize several of these investing styles at a given time and is not restricted to any particular investment approach or asset class.
Expected Volatility: Variable

Multi Strategy:
Investment approach is diversified by employing various strategies simultaneously to realize short- and long-term gains. Other strategies may include systems trading such as trend following and various diversified technical strategies. This style of investing allows the manager to overweight or underweight different strategies to best capitalize on current investment opportunities.
Expected Volatility: Variable

Short Selling:
Sells securities short in anticipation of being able to rebuy them at a future date at a lower price due to the manager's assessment of the overvaluation of the securities, or the market, or in anticipation of earnings disappointments often due to accounting irregularities, new competition, change of management, etc. Often used as a hedge to offset long-only portfolios and by those who feel the market is approaching a bearish cycle. High risk.
Expected Volatility: Very High

Special Situations:
Invests in event-driven situations such as mergers, hostile takeovers, reorganizations, or leveraged buyouts. May involve simultaneous purchase of stock in companies being acquired, and the sale of stock in its acquirer, hoping to profit from the spread between the current market price and the ultimate purchase price of the company. May also utilize derivatives to leverage returns and to hedge out interest rate and/or market risk. Results generally not dependent on direction of market.
Expected Volatility: Moderate

Value:
Invests in securities perceived to be selling at deep discounts to their intrinsic or potential worth. Such securities may be out of favor or underfollowed by analysts. Long-term holding, patience, and strong discipline are often required until the ultimate value is recognized by the market.
Expected Volatility: Low – Moderate

About Jason Mitchell

Jason Mitchell is the stimulating, truth-telling modern Renaissance Man; a serial, successful entrepreneur; trusted marketing advisor, singer, consultant and coach to hundreds of private entrepreneurial clients running businesses from $5-million to $10-billion in size.

As a speaker, Jason delivers content that enriches, inspires, changes, and challenges all those in attendance.

An expert on topics such as investing, real estate, personal development, relationships, sex, life, spirituality, and self improvement Jason is never without something to say and share that leaves his audience feeling like they have earned more than their money's worth.

As a singer, Jason is asked to perform in a number of genres and styles. From gospel to rock, jazz to blues, opera to musicals, R&B to Pop Jason leaves the crowd wanting more, and always gives his absolute best. Jason takes on corporate gigs, music festivals, and other venues commanding top fees from those who want a professional.

When you call Jason, you get a rich deep bass-baritone voice that leaves you remembering his name and feeling like part of the family. Mostly doing private parties and events getting paid upward of $50,000 to $75,000 Jason only takes on gigs where he can add value, leave a lasting impression, and where he feels he can give his clients the best.

As a direct-response marketing consultant and copywriter, Jason is the "secret sauce" behind full-page magazine ads, TV infomercials, online marketing and direct mail. He is routinely paid upwards from $50,000.00 to, on average, $100,000.00 to $200,000.00 plus royalties to create direct-response ads, sales letters, direct-mail campaigns and integrated offline/online marketing systems for his private clients…

He has created winning campaigns for health, diet and beauty products and companies, B2B and industry products including software, and the finance and investment markets — Jason does a massive amount of work in the information-marketing industry including book, home study course, online course and newsletter publishers; seminar, conference and event promoters; coaching organizations; and associations. Most new client relationships begin with an initial consulting day at his base fee of $20,000.00, conducted in one of his homes, or $40,000 if you want him to come to you. There is usually a waiting list, and new client candidates are asked to communicate initially via a one to two page memo describing their business, needs and interests.

To see about hiring Jason for work as a consultant for your business, to manage your portfolio, or anything else e-mail jakm86@gmail.com and your request will be processed and you will be alerted as to the next step.